Productivity

Improving Productivity
Increasing Productivity
Discover How To Mastermind Your Life For Peak Performance Success

By Ace McCloud
Copyright © 2014

Disclaimer

The information provided in this book is designed to provide helpful information on the subjects discussed. This book is not meant to be used, nor should it be used, to diagnose or treat any medical condition. For diagnosis or treatment of any medical problem, consult your own physician. The author is not responsible for any health needs that may require medical supervision and is not liable for any damages or negative consequences from any treatment, action, application or preparation, to any person reading or following the information in this book. Readers should be aware that any websites or links listed in this book may change.

Table of Contents

Introduction 6
Chapter 1: What is Productivity and Why is it So Important? 7
Chapter 2: More Energy = More Productivity 9
Chapter 3: The Best Productivity Boosting Habits............ 13
Chapter 4: Strategies to Become More Productive 18
Chapter 5: The Top Productivity Tools 24
Chapter 6: How Productivity Can Change Your Life.......... 26
Conclusion 28
My Other Books and Audio Books 29

Be sure to check out my website for all my Books and Audio books.

www.AcesEbooks.com

Introduction

I want to thank you and congratulate you for buying the book, "Ultimate Productivity: How To Improve Productivity, Develop Productivity, Manage Productivity, And Acquire The Right Tools To Be Supremely Productive At Work And Home."

In this book you will discover how to overcome procrastination at work and at home, including tips on how to maintain your physical and mental health for improved productivity. You will also learn about habits and strategies that will help you be more productive so that you can start crushing the competition. Some more things that you will discover include the top tools for increased productivity and how to bring everything together so that you can live to your full potential! If you've been putting off a large project or if you just want to learn how to live a more efficient and fulfilling lifestyle, this book will serve as your trusted guide for getting you performing at peak levels. You are about to discover just how simple it is to improve your levels of productivity in any area of life that you choose to focus on!

Chapter 1: What is Productivity and Why is it So Important?

Procrastination: we've all experienced it. Many of us have put off something important in our lives—whether it was a school assignment, a personal goal, or a project for work. The thought that you *don't* have to work hard on something makes it easy for us to put important things off. Many things other than our personal and work projects often seem more appealing to us, such as watching a movie or mindlessly surfing the web. However, as small as procrastination seems, it can have a very negative effect on our lives, especially if it becomes a habit. The more we allow ourselves to procrastinate, the less productive our lives become.

Productivity is very important and it has many definitions. I like to view productivity as what we get when we divide value by time. Technically speaking, there are two ways of looking at productivity. If you can get good value from spending a lot of time on a task, then you have achieved productivity and if you can complete one or more tasks quickly then you've just added a valuable resource to your day—time. Most importantly, the sooner you start saving time, the more you can accomplish during your lifespan. More procrastination equals more wasted time. Being productive is important for everyone. Whether you are a businessperson, a student, or if you work from home, productivity is a very important factor in your life.

Productivity is healthy for our bodies and mind and procrastination can actually lead to some unhealthy habits. First and foremost, procrastination causes us to become extra stressed out and will cause us to put off important tasks until the last-minute. Procrastination can encourage laziness as well. Once you are in that lazy frame of mind, it makes it less likely that you will exercise, eat properly and get the important things that you should be doing accomplished. Procrastination can also cause your work to be sloppy because when you actually get around to doing it, you may be limited on time causing you to skip corners and make mistakes that you normally would not have made. If you get into the habit of procrastination, it can follow you throughout the rest of your personal and work life. If you promise your employer that you will get something done and you don't, you can damage your credibility. If you prove untrustworthy to your family and friends, you may also end up with damaged relationships. Most of all, life is short, so, to make the most of it, try and lead a productive lifestyle.

By becoming more productive in all areas of life, more people will begin to trust and rely on you. Being productive is also an excellent way to set and reach goals so that you can make the most of out of your life. Being strategically productive will give you the greatest chance of accomplishing your dreams and desires. Best of all, anybody can make their lives more productive. Productivity is not exclusive—as long as you commit to making some big or small life changes, you can be much more successful.

The rest of this book will show you proven and effective ways to boost your daily productivity. It will cover the topic of energy and how it contributes to productivity, productivity-boosting habits and strategies that you can practice, productivity-boosting items that you can start out with, and how to combine everything together to live an incredibly productive life. This book also includes specific examples that will help you put productivity into perspective. If you have a history of procrastination and you're ready for a change, prepare yourself to learn the secrets to beating procrastination and boosting your personal performance.

Chapter 2: More Energy = More Productivity

In order to live a productive life, the first action you should take is to reevaluate your physical and mental health status. For high levels of productivity, your body must have high levels of energy. Low levels of energy can cause us to feel tired and sluggish, lowering the chances of getting things done. Low levels of energy can also tempt us to stay in bed all day or to put off important tasks until the last-minute. Everybody's levels of energy are different, depending on what they eat, their schedule, genetics and their habits. If you often find yourself wishing that you had more energy and a higher drive, then stop wishing because you can—by following some of the upcoming tips, learn how to boost your energy levels and become more productive in all areas of your life.

Become More Energetic By Changing Your Diet

The better your diet, the more likely you are to be energized. Having more energy means being more productive. Many of us try to mask our sluggish periods with energy drinks and energy snacks—this will actually give you the opposite of what you want over the long term. The best way to naturally boost your levels of energy is to eat foods that contain energizing nutrients—ones that your body can convert to energy on its own. To become more energetic, you should try to factor in plenty of whole grains, protein-packed foods, fruits and vegetables, and lean meat into your diet. Those types of food contain proteins, fiber, iron, omega-3 fatty acids, B vitamins, Vitamin A, Vitamin C, Vitamin E, and Magnesium, all of which help your body convert food to energy. You can eat these foods individually or you can combine them into meals for a greater boost of energy. Also, try to avoid foods that contain high levels of sugar or drinks that contain caffeine.

It is also very helpful to eat smaller, easily digested meals. Just breaking up your food intake from 3 large meals to 4-5 smaller meals can make a huge difference. One of the best habits I have gotten into is to have a fruit and vegetable smoothie every morning upon waking up along with a large glass of water. It digests quickly, gives good energy, and kick starts your metabolism. The Nutribullet blender is great for this. You will usually feel hungry just a few hours later, and this is a great time for a light snack, such as almonds, which are great for energy!

Physical Exercise

Exercising for a certain amount of time for three days a week will naturally boost your body's energy levels. A simple exercise, such as a brisk walk in the morning, will help strengthen your heart, causing it to pump more oxygen, which helps your body create more energy. You should try to factor in plenty of cardio and strength training exercises into your weekly workout routine. The ideal amount of workout time per day is 30 minutes to an hour based on what type of workout you are doing, and you should try to work out four or more days in the week. Many people manage their time by waking up early to schedule in a workout.

You can start to factor in physical exercise to your schedule by making small changes, like opting to climb more stairs or parking further away from your destination in a parking lot.

Mental Exercise

Productivity requires having a sense of mental clarity. Without a clear mind, it is hard to stay organized and motivated. Not only is mental clarity important for having more levels of energy, it also gives you a sense of direction in your life. Many people wait for mental clarity to magically happen but it will not. You should try to keep your mind clear every day.

You can practice mental clarity by simply taking a break from all of your work. Some of the more popular options include doing some yoga and meditation, which serve as great methods of relaxation. This YouTube video, Learn how to meditate by Meditation Videos, shows how to practice meditation for a completely clear mind. It is a good watch for beginners. I would also recommend Hypnosis Downloads for an incredible variety of incredible downloads. Some of my favorites include: Develop Self Discipline, Reach Your Goals, Success Motivation, energy booster and many more.

Listening to relaxing music can also help you focus in many cases. Here is a great YouTube video by relaxingrecords composed of relaxing music that can help you focus: Brain Music - STUDY FOCUS CONCENTRATE.

Get a Good Night's Sleep

The amount of work that you can get done in a day is directly correlated with how much sleep we get. If you only sleep for three hours one night and then you have to get up and go to work, you know how hard it is to get through the day. In fact, you will probably end up going to bed early that night and sleeping in the next day—hours that you could be using to get something done. To stay energized throughout the day, you should be certain to get enough sleep. The standard amount of sleep for adults is eight hours a night. You should also get into the habit of going to bed early and waking up early. By getting up early, you can fit in at least two or three more hours' worth of activities.

For example, if you go to bed by 9pm and wake up at 5am (thus getting a full eight hours of sleep), and you have to be at work by 8am, you have at least 2 ½ hours to shower, eat breakfast, work out, spend time with your family, or to get extra work done. Finally, you should practice staying consistent with your sleeping habits. If you decide to wake up early during the week, do it on the weekends too. If you allow yourself to slip up your sleep schedule for even a day or two, your body's energy levels can easily get lowered and you will find it more difficult to get back into your optimum healthy routine.

Take Vitamins and Supplements

Another way to increase your energy levels is to take vitamins and supplements. These substances are especially good for those who may have a vitamin/nutrient deficiency. One solution is to take natural supplements, depending on what kind(s) of nutrients your body needs most. This section lists some of the best vitamins and supplements that you can take to boost your energy levels.

Multivitamins

Multivitamins are a great type of vitamin to take for energy because they provide your body with all the nutrients it needs in one dose. Multivitamins are also great because there are specific kinds for women, men, and kids to ensure that people of all ages and genders can keep themselves healthy. They are often easy to swallow and most people prefer to take them as they eat breakfast. For men, I highly recommend the Optimum Nutrition Opti-Men Multivitamins brand. This multivitamin brings together 75 active ingredients, including B vitamins and amino acids, to provide your body with the right amount of energy that it needs to be productive. For women, I highly recommend the same brand: Optimum Nutrition Opti-Women Multivitamins. This multivitamin is nearly the same as the kind for men, except that it has 40 active ingredients and 17 special ingredients that are specific to the female body.

Omega-3 Fatty Acids

Omega-3 fatty acids are one nutrient that our bodies can convert to energy. We usually get this nutrient in the form of seafood. However, many people are unable to eat seafood because of allergies or just because they don't like it. In that case, a great way to provide our bodies with this nutrient is through a supplement. One of my favorite omega-3 fatty acid supplements is Kirkland Natural Fish Oil. I especially like this one because it brings together oil from several fish: anchovies, salmon, herring, soy, sprat, and sardine. It's also all natural because it doesn't contain any artificial products.

Coenzyme Q10

Our bodies naturally produce coenzyme Q10, a substance that helps our energy molecules recharge, but some peoples' bodies are unable to produce it. Specifically, many people with AIDS, high blood pressure, and heart failure tend to have a coenzyme Q10 deficiency. One of the best supplements for this substance is Nature's Bounty Co Q10. It serves as an antioxidant, which will keep your heart strong and provide you with more energy. It also brings energy to your muscles and brain, making it an excellent energy supplement.

Ginseng

Ginseng is a natural substance that helps physically and mentally energize our bodies, especially when we are under stress. Ginseng is a great supplement for those who get easily drained from overworking. If you are a procrastinator who is looking to become more productive, ginseng might be a good supplement to use to help start off your change. I highly recommend using Irwins Natural Ginza Plus Endurance. This product will give you plenty of energy and has no side effects, unlike other supplements or medications may bring on. It does not contain any stimulants either, making it an all-natural product.

Focus Formula
To get in the mood to focus before doing work or other important things, I would recommend Focus Formula, it is fairly inexpensive and works great.

There is a lot more you can do to all naturally increase your energy. If you would like more energy in your life then I would highly recommend my bestselling book: **Ultimate Energy**.

Chapter 3: The Best Productivity Boosting Habits

At some point in your life, you have probably formed a bad habit or know someone who has formed a bad habit. Many times, people label habits as bad and not good. However, habits can actually be very good, especially for boosting productivity. Forming habits is important because they are the foundation for setting and reaching goals. In this chapter, you will learn some very good productivity-boosting habits. Most importantly, we call habits 'habits' because they tend to stick with us—and as long as you form some good, productivity-boosting habits, you will likely be able to utilize them throughout your entire life.

Learn Time Management Skills

By getting into some routine, productivity-improving habits, you can increase your productivity at work and at home. Some of these habits are good for increasing productivity in the short-term, but by sticking to good habits, these tips will stick with you for weeks, months, and years to come. Having good time management skills is one of the best productivity-boosting habits to get into. By being able to prioritize your time, you will find yourself able to better manage your tasks and you might even come out with some free time for yourself once you get really good at it.

The first step to learning time management skills is to be aware of how important time is. Then, you should become aware of how much time you spend on your tasks. If you are working on a task that you've never done before, make a note of what time you start and set a deadline for yourself. If you are working on tasks that you are familiar with, you will become familiar with how long they take you and it will be easier to manage time. All in all, there are many ways to practice good time management skills and the more you practice them, the quicker they will become second-nature to you. This chapter suggests some good habits that you can practice to learn how to utilize your time more effectively.

Ask For Help

Whether at home or at work, nobody should have to do everything themselves. For example, if you are in charge of getting a huge project at work done, you shouldn't be afraid to delegate tasks to your co-workers. If you are looking to increase your productivity at home, you can ask your family members or roommates for help, too. For example, if you need help rearranging furniture, asking someone else to help you will get the job done twice as fast and leave more time and energy to do something else. Many people do not ask others for help because of trust issues and shyness. Many people do not trust others to get a task done as well as they know they will get it done themselves. Others are often simply too shy to ask, hoping for help that never comes. If you decide to ask someone for help as a way to improve your productivity, pick someone who you have the utmost confidence in, someone you can count on, and someone whom you feel comfortable asking. Be sure to return the favor, and with a trusted relationship, you will be much more productive in the future.

To-Do Lists

By making to-do lists, you can help yourself become more organized and you will also be able to visualize your workload. To-do lists help you stay more organized because you can cross off the tasks that you've completed until you've crossed everything off. By creating a to-do list, you will no longer have to rely on your memory to memorize everything that you need to get done.

There are two great ways to make to-do lists. You can create them manually, with a traditional pad and paper, or you can go digital. Many people who have smart phones use the features of their phones to make notes for themselves. If you have a smart phone, there are many different kinds of free applications that you can download to aid yourself in creating a to-do list.

You may find yourself spending more or less time on one task than you would like. This YouTube video by eHow shows you how to write and use an effective to-do list and serves as a great introduction to a productivity-boosting strategy that I will be covering in the next chapter: Writing Lessons: How to Write an Effective To Do List.

For important tasks, I have small squares of white paper cut up in a large pile. I will then take one of the pieces of paper and write down my idea or goal that needs to be accomplished. Over the course of time, it is easy for these to pile up. I will be sure to take the most important tasks that need to be accomplished and put them on the center of my desk in the order that they should be completed for optimum efficiency. When the task is done, I take great pleasure in throwing the piece of paper away (if the other side isn't empty) and moving onto the next most important task. For all the other ideas that are on pieces of paper that may be less important at the moment, but something you definitely want to do in the future, just tape them into a notebook or binder that you can review later when you have more time. It can be extremely overwhelming if your home or workplace is filled with notes on things to do, so consolidating them is usually a good idea.

Take a Break

For those of you who sit at a desk for most of the day, you may notice that your energy levels easily drain. This is because our fat cells tend to build up in our bodies when we sit for a long time. Fat cells drain us of our energy, making us less productive. It also generally has a negative impact on our health. One good way to stay energized throughout your work day is to take a break from sitting down. Get up, walk around, and let your mind clear from your work. At home, it is also good to take breaks. If you do so much work at home that your mind begins to fog, do the same: get up, take a walk or do something fun, and let your mind rejuvenate. It is never a good idea to focus on one task for too long—your mind and body will eventually get drained out and you will not perform as well or as fast as you would without giving it a rest. You can utilize your break time to eat a healthy snack, take a brisk walk, take a nap, listen to a hypnosis download, or do something else that will complement your productivity. If you find yourself under a lot of stress or just want more laugher and joy in your life, then I would highly recommend my book: Laughter and Humor Therapy.

Disconnect from Distractions

Today, technology is around us wherever we go. Most of us have smart phones, computers, high-definition TVs, and endless social media websites to choose from. All this technology is great, but sometimes they can be very distracting. It is likely that you or someone you know is constantly checking their phone or computer for an email, a Facebook update, or something similar.

Distractions like those can decrease the levels of productivity in all of us, whether we are a student, a homebody, or a workaholic. For example, one study shows that the average college student will spend one more hour per day on social media than they spend on studying. One great way to disconnect from these distractions is to shut them off—you can easily disable social media accounts (with the option to turn them back on at a later date), unplug your TVs, take the batteries out of your remotes, and uninstall distracting apps from your phones. One great thing about technology is that you can usually turn off your distractions without losing any of the information that you store in them.

On the topic of checking email, you should limit yourself to checking your email to one or two times per day. Many of us, especially those in the business world, have the tendency to constantly check emails—time that you could be using toward something more productive, like the most important thing on your to do list. By designating a certain amount of time for email, you can still effectively manage your communication while making more time for more important tasks. If you receive many emails per day, you might even try to see if you can set your phone up where it will play a sound any time you get an email—that way, you will not have to waste time checking it only to find out that you don't have anything new.

Focus and Avoid Interruptions

The best method to get things done is to try and focus on one task at a time, especially if your tasks are not related. You should also stay working on it until it's completely finished. Again, turn off all distractions to make this habit easier. If you switch between too many tasks without finishing them, it is easier to become confused and you may forget the important points of each task. One thing that you can do to help you remain focused is to avoid interruptions as much as possible. You can avoid interruptions by simply closing your office door, turning off your phone, or just ignoring other distractions while you focus on what is most important. Studies show that when you are interrupted from doing something, you risk an 80% chance of not getting back to it at all.

Learning how to say no also comes in handy for this habit. Saying no is not easy, especially when it comes to our close friends, family, and bosses, but sometimes you have to bite the bullet and do it. However, saying no doesn't have to be a dreadful thing. For example, if somebody calls you and asks you to hang out, do not give in to temptation—simply reschedule the request. It will save you time, help you focus, and it will motivate you to get your tasks done because it gives you something to look forward too. I know just how hard saying no can be for some people but this YouTube video How To Say "No!" to Almost Anything by Epipheo is a great motivator for saying no and contains some handy tips on putting it in perspective.

Set Challenging, Realistic Goals

If you want to see a boost in your productivity, you should get into the habit of setting goals. The best thing about goals is that there are two types: short-term and long-term. If you are unsure of whether you should set goals for yourself, think back to your to-do lists—if you're completing all of your tasks within a few hours or within a day, you might want to start challenging yourself a bit more. You might also have something that you want to accomplish in one day—that can be a goal, too. Goal setting also encourages motivation, which in turn encourages productivity. Studies show that those who set goals for themselves are happier than those without goals. Goal setting requires the combination of time management and organization. It encourages productivity because you will have to work hard to reach your goal(s). One good way to start is to set some daily goals for yourself. Plan out your daily goals the day or the night before so that you have time to prepare yourself for them the next day. This will also give your brain some time to sort things through while you sleep. By setting short-term goals, you can eventually set and achieve long-term goals.

Follow Up On Your Goals

Most of us are aware that goal-setting is easy—actually going through with achieving your goals is the hard part. Distractions and overall laziness often tempt us to state our goals and then put them off until a later date. By taking immediate action to work toward your goals, you will have a better chance at achieving them. You should also read through your goals every day! Making excuses is a common flaw that many of us tend to have but we can overcome it by actively taking steps toward our goals. Instead of wishing that you could do something, just put your fears aside and do it. Fear is often a huge reason why many people don't achieve the level of success they could have. The reality is, what you fear may be so horrible, in many cases, isn't that bad at all. Hypnosis Downloads has an incredible download on this called: Overcome Fear of Failure.

Give yourself a head start, even if you are unsure about how well your goals are planned out—you can always work that part out along the way. Following up on your goals will make you more productive because the more you get done, the more you learn and you can apply what you learn to different areas of your life.

For example, if you wish that you could learn a new language, do something about it: take a class or buy some language-learning software. Then, make a commitment to it and follow through. Once you successfully learn the language, you can use it to help other people with translations, you can travel to a country where it is the main language, and you can add it to your resume, which may increase your chances at getting a new or better job. The possibilities are endless when you follow up on your goals.

If you are truly serious about accomplishing a goal, tell other people about it who you respect. It is always extremely disappointing to tell people you care about or respect that you have failed, so this can be an added motivator to accomplish the goal. You can also recruit a friend or family member as an accountability partner, someone who will hold you to a higher standard to see if you accomplish your goal or not. For many, just the shame of failing will motivate them to succeed, but if not, you can always award a penalty for failure, collected by the accountability partner. It's sort of basic, but can definitely motivate.

Give Yourself a Reward

Finally, there is nothing better than getting something nice for working hard all week. Rewarding yourself for hard work gives you something to look forward too and will help motivate you to get all of your work done. It is similar to taking a break, but your reward can be a little bigger. Remember when you unplugged your TV and disabled your social media profiles? Allow yourself to reconnect to these things when you have completed all the work you need to get done or after you've reached one of your goals. If you want to really reward yourself, you could plan a trip or vacation for you and your family, which will net you quality time and a relaxing break from your regular work.

Chapter 4: Strategies to Become More Productive

Once you get into the practice of learning how to stick to good, productive habits, you can use those habits to try out some productivity-boosting strategies. There are many kinds of strategies to become more productive and, since everybody is different, you will have to experiment and see which strategies work best for you. However, by following some of these upcoming strategies, you can get much more done in much less time. Some of these strategies are short-term but many of them can easily turn into long-term strategies that will change your life.

The 80/20 Rule

A principle known as the 80/20 rule follows the theory that 20% of your daily actions produces 80% of the results that you get. To be a little more specific, by focusing on the most critical 20% of something, you will get the highest quality results. Anything else that you do doesn't have that much effect on the final results. The idea of the 80/20 rule is to encourage people to learn how to identify the most important parts of your tasks. This way, you can focus on those parts when your physical and mental energy levels are at their highest.

Establish a Morning Routine

Establishing a morning routine is a great strategy for making your days more productive. Having a routine that you follow every morning after you wake up can benefit you in many ways. You will find yourself more organized and with plenty of extra time to spare later on. Second, it can help your body get used to waking up at a certain time, which will ultimately give you more energy to use throughout the day. Third, it is good for your overall health, especially when you incorporate good health practices into it, like stretching, eating healthy, exercising, and mind preparation techniques.

Since we all work different jobs and have different schedules and responsibilities, nobody's morning routine will be exactly the same. You will have to create it yourself based upon your daily lifestyle. Some people may choose to wake up early and do yoga for more energy. Other people may prefer to get some daily tasks out-of-the-way, such as checking their email or doing laundry. Again, depending on your life and your responsibilities, this part is entirely up to you. You should always try to make breakfast a part of your morning routine, since breakfast will give your body an energy boost, which will help increase your productivity.

Fill in Time Gaps

One way to seriously boost your productivity is to fill in any time gaps that you have. Time gaps are any miscellaneous periods of time that are too short to get an entire task done but long enough to do something productive. For example, if you are waiting for a client to call you back after your conversation is interrupted, use that spare time to read up on something or to prepare your next big task. You will be surprised at how much more you can get done when you utilize all of the time gaps throughout your day.

Monitor Yourself

By monitoring your goals and your progress on them, you can easily keep track of your performance. This strategy can be short-term or long-term. Monitor your goals at work and at home by keeping track of reports, reviews, or by keeping your own notes. You can incorporate the habit of following up on your goals to use as your main motivator for keeping track of your performance. By keeping track of your goals, you can review your progress to see where you need to make improvements and where you are excelling. Reviewing goals daily is an excellent habit that many of the greatest people in the world do habitually.

Recognize Your Strengths

One amazing (and relatively logical) strategy for increasing productivity is to focus and work on your strengths. This strategy is best for people who are already established in a career and not those who are still exploring what they are good at and what kind of career is a good fit for them. By focusing on your strengths, you can get tasks done much quicker. For example, if you're a writer by profession, you should focus on writing material and not trying to come up with cover art for the book cover. If you have many talents but you're extra good at one particular talent, use it to your ability, whether at work or at home. Some of the most successful and highly paid people in the world just specialize in one thing, and do it incredibly well!

Your talents are not the same as your strengths. Strengths are abilities that you were naturally born with—anyone can learn a talent if they work really hard at it. For example, anybody can learn how to play the drums, but not many people are naturally good at solving math problems.

By identifying your strengths, you can use them to determine what kind of career you will excel in or what kind of business you might be really good at. Also, using your strengths on your tasks and projects will make them more enjoyable, which will make you work faster and happier. If you are truly unsure of how to identify your strengths, this YouTube video, 5 Questions to Discover Your Strengths by Jonathan Milligan, uses five questions that you can ask yourself to help figure it out.

Differentiate Between "Perfect" and "Complete"

Many people are perfectionists but they do not realize how much of a time-waster perfectionism can be. Contrary to popular belief, perfectionism does not always drive successful results. A fully completed project will almost always get better results than a perfect but incomplete project. You should also be able to differentiate between perfect results and polished results. You can always go back and edit, update, or revise your project or task.

If you cannot go back and change things, then it is important that you do a quality job the first time. While it can be advantageous in some instances to get a project complete, if it will hurt your reputation, then it is almost always better to make sure it is done correctly the first time. It doesn't have to be perfect, but it should be quality. After all, in business and in life, your reputation is everything.

I personally lean towards more of a perfectionist standard, which can be time draining at times, but I get incredible joy when a project is done, knowing that it will stand the test of time.

Set Deadlines and Appropriate Standards

Setting deadlines is a very effective strategy for increasing productivity. When you have a deadline for a project or a task, you are aware of when you need to finish it and how long you have to finish it. Without a deadline, it is easy for us to forget about projects and tasks and it's even easier for us to put them off. If you are working on something for someone else, promise them a due date. If you are working on a personal task, promise yourself a date by which you will get it done. Also, try to set appropriate standards for your task. Do not try to associate your task with high, unreachable standards. Set the standards at a realistic and reachable rate. You can supplement this strategy with the habit of getting into writing a to-do list or keeping a planner to help you keep track of your deadlines.

Training

For those who want to increase their workplace productivity, think about the training you and your co-workers have received. Your boss may have only trained you on one aspect of your job and not another. By cross-training employees, an organization or company can be responsible for getting tasks done and complete them at a much quicker pace. If you think that your company or organization can benefit from cross-training, don't be afraid to suggest it to your boss or supervisor. If you're the owner of business, consider cross-training your employees for increasing productivity.

Combine Like Tasks

Check your to-do list and look for any basic tasks that you can get done at once. For the most part, this is also called multitasking. At work, you could try to take on several projects at once if they are about similar topics. Some people suggest that multitasking will actually make you less productive, but the trick is to be logical about it. For example, you would not try to write a book chapter while taking an important phone call.

Get Rid of Clutter

Did you know that clutter can actually cause you to become stressed out? It's also a huge time-waster, especially when it causes you to spend more time looking for paperwork, your keys, your phone, or anything else you might need to complete your tasks. These two points alone show that reducing the clutter in your environment can boost your productivity. By putting some time aside to clean up your environment, whether it's your workspace or your house, you can actually save yourself time in the future. I had a huge printer and Xerox in my office for many years, but hardly ever used it anymore once I got my color printer. It was a huge relief when I finally sold it and cleared up the space for more Zen like things. When you are getting ready to work, get rid of all distractions, and just surround yourself with the items needed to complete the task. For an added bonus, try decorating your home or your office with some live plants—they generate oxygen and they look pretty too.

Organization

It is always good to be organized. It is nice to know exactly where everything is quickly and easily. For the computer, one of my favorite programs is: Microsoft OneNote. This program is incredible for organizing a massive amount of information; it can be accessed quickly, and allows you to just have one program open instead of many more, which can quickly get confusing. Another great organizing tool for the computer is: Anytime Organizer. For the home and workplace, try and combine things into folders, shelves, notebooks, bookcases, and other similar items that allow you to easily organize your possessions in an efficient manner.

Break Up Large Tasks

If you have a really big task and you cannot get help from anyone, try to break it down into smaller tasks. This way, you will not get overwhelmed by the stress of it and you won't burn out your mental energy worrying about the enormity of the task. For example, an author might write a book one chapter at a time until he or she is done, a home builder will just focus on building project at a time, a world class athlete will just focus on one workout or one completion at a time. Breaking up large tasks into small tasks requires combining the habits of keeping a to-do list/planner and learning time management habits along with keeping up your energy and continually feeding yourself inspiration and motivation.

Visualization

This is a critical skill that should be developed by everyone. It is simple to do and study after study has shown it to be one of the most effective skills for reaching goals and being supremely productive. Whenever you have some free time, just visualize in your head the goal you want to accomplish. Go through this goal from beginning to end, seeing yourself accomplishing each step successfully, and then try and really get the feeling of joy and victory as you visualize yourself accomplishing this goal. If you would like to improve your visualization skills, HypnosisDownloads has a great download called: Improve Visualization.

Surround Yourself With Other Productive People

One great way to boost your productivity is to surround yourself with happy, upbeat, and positive people. Specifically, if you surround yourself with other productive people, you will feel more productivity-boosting motivation. Try to avoid negative people who try to bring you down and discourage you—this may only tack on extra time being stressed out. If you are just learning how to improve your productivity, networking with other successfully productive people at meetings, workshops, and events is a great way to learn and to make professional connections. If you don't work or you need to improve your home-life productivity more than your work-life productivity, think about productive friends or family members that you can ask for advice and look up too as mentors.

Recharge Your Battery

Recharge your battery with uplifting and positive images, videos, quotes, books, movies, music and other things that will keep you motivated and trying to achieve. Tony Robbins is always a good investment in my opinion, Hypnosis Downloads is incredible, the "Be More Productive" download is a good choice, and their "Stellar Success" program is really powerful. In many cases, you can find some inspiration and motivation for free online. My favorite place for this is YouTube. Below are some great inspirational, healing, and motivational videos from YouTube.

Six Secrets To Success
Tony Robbins On Focus
Healing And Forgiveness
I am a Champion
How Great I Am
The Best Motivation - Productivity
The Difference Between A Winner And A Loser

Find out what motivates you and be sure to use it on a consistent basis to help keep your productivity batteries charged.

Don't Rush

Finally, don't rush through anything. Trying to get things done too fast may have some negative outcomes. Your work's quality may suffer if you try to fly through a task too quickly. Speed can also cause stress and anxiety, which can actually drain your mental energy and make you less productive. A good way to keep yourself paced is to tackle one task at a time. Do the most important things first and save the easy ones for last—saving the best for last also serves as an incentive because you will not have to work as hard in the end.

To be truly productive you will need Influence, Willpower, And Discipline. If you are serious about being supremely productive and living the best life you possibly can, then be sure to read my bestselling book: [Influence, Willpower, And Discipline](#).

Chapter 5: The Top Productivity Tools

As you know from reading this book so far, you can increase your productivity by planning out your days, making to-do lists, and writing down your goals. One great way to make sure that you have all of this information together at the tip of your fingers is to invest in an agenda or planner book. Many stores carry basic versions of planners, but for bringing out the most productivity in your life, I highly recommend the Plan Ahead Home/Office 18-Months Planner. This planner is an all-in-one tool: it comes with a reference calendar for four years and math tools such as conversion tables and a time-zone map. It's best features are the four tabbed dividers. Each tab is for planning, contacts, resources, and notes. With this planner, you can organize your tasks from day-to-day, write notes for yourself, and have instant access to your contacts and any other important information that you need. The dates cover an 18-month period, so you can plan your days out months advance. Finally, this product is relatively small, portable, and durable, so it is perfect to carry with you all the time.

For your computer, an excellent program is: Anytime Organizer. This software will alert you with a sound and pop up when important events or tasks are at hand, and has a ton of other great features.

Another great agenda/planner, specifically for working on your goal-setting skills, is the 90 Days Goal Planner Life Coach. This planner covers 90 days and is designed to help people become more productive and achieve their goals.

If you do not need an extensive planner but you still want to practice writing to-do lists and other notes to help you become more productive, another great productivity-boosting product is the Wear-N-Write Clip-On Dry Erase Notepad. This product is especially handy for people who are constantly on the move, such as contractors, business managers, students, and more. This product is small and clips almost anywhere, so you can hang it in your car, office, or even wear it on your belt to remind yourself of important dates, phone numbers, tasks and meetings. It is a perfect tool to help you stay organized and productive.

For those who want to time themselves on tasks to learn better time management, I highly recommend buying a timer. You can use a timer to set time goals for completing tasks and projects. You can also use a timer to learn how to pick up your pace. One of the best timers for boosting productivity is the Multifunction LCD Alarm Clock. This product is perfect for anyone who is looking to become more productive. Not only does it serve as a timer/alarm clock, it is also a pen holder, an envelope-opener, a calendar, and even a thermometer. If you work at a desk, this product is a must-have—you will never have to take an extra walk to get a pen, open a piece of mail, or check the weather. This product is also relatively small and portable so you can take it with you wherever you are working.

For ultimate organization, one strategy that has worked for many people is to invest in a tablet computer. Tablet computers are very small and portable and function just like a computer. Tablet computers are good for anyone looking to boost their productivity. You can download many free and paid applications to your tablet to help you stay organized and efficient. Many developers have released to-do list apps, timer apps, file-sharing apps, and even apps where you can quickly access your bank accounts, quickly find a local business, and read the news.

Most tablet computers also have built-in contact lists, video chat applications, and alarms. With a tablet computer, you will have access to many productive tools in one little electronic device. While some tablet computers are very expensive, there are many high-quality ones that are reasonably cheap and work great. One of the best tablet computers currently is the Samsung Galaxy Tab 3. This tablet computer is not too expensive and comes with plenty of memory and even 50 free gigabytes of file-sharing storage. It also has a built-in front and rear camera, which is perfect for telecommunication. You can connect it to the internet and surf the web using the free wi-fi function. However, the Kindle Fire HDX is my favorite! It is a beast, and built to smash the competition. Another good idea is to download some productivity boosting apps to your computer, smart phone, or your tablet.

Chapter 6: How Productivity Can Change Your Life

Now that you have made it this far, it is time to learn how to combine all of the habits and strategies that you have learned to lead the most ultimately of productive lifestyles. I encourage you to practice all of the tips that I have covered in this book to see what is the best strategic fit for you. Be sure to make the activities that give you the best results a habit that you follow every day.

It can be very easy to put things off or let the fear of failure paralyze you into inaction or unhealthy habits. Being productive doesn't *mean* that your life has to be overwhelming. Chunk things down, be smart with your time, and it is always important to remember that inspiration and motivation is fleeting. So **pounce** when the ***inspiration*** arises and be sure to do the things mentioned earlier in this book to keep on replenishing your drive and motivation. It would be incredible if you could just do one thing and be motivated forever. The truth is, you need to nourish and strengthen this drive within you constantly to keep getting peak performance results.

When I was a pro gamer, reaching levels of domination it would take pages for me to explain and a world top player in the number one game in the world with over 25 million players, I used to take horrible care of my body. I would go to bed and wake up whenever I wanted. My eating habits where sloppy and so was my exercise routine. However, I did take a nice long walk every day, which is one of the best things for health that you can do. When I finally had accomplished my goal of being a World top player, I felt that I had no direction or purpose in life and that I could be doing more with my life.

My most important changes started with my sleeping habits. I made a promise to myself to start becoming more disciplined with my sleep times. It didn't take me long to get used to my new sleeping routine and I found myself with enough extra time to prepare a more healthy breakfast in the morning. I started to stock my kitchen with healthy foods like fresh strawberries, blueberries, apples, bananas, whole grain breads, yogurts, spinach, asparagus, pork loins, and skinless chicken. I also invested heavily in healthy supplements and personal development cd's.

Then, I started to do my bodybuilding routine that I had been doing for the previous fifteen years but had neglected for almost two years straight, along with my daily walking routine. For my work, I bought a planner and set aside extra time each day to plan out my week. Being able to see the dates and the entire week right in front of me helped me plan and set deadline for my projects. Luckily, the planner that I chose had a section for goals. My first goal was to learn how to become independent from my main distraction: the internet and video games. In the past, I always left my social media sites and messengers open, so I was constantly connected to other peoples' lives, but not my own. Again, I gathered up my willpower, gathered up everything I needed to work, and then would just open the things that would help me accomplish the task at hand, and close everything else. I couldn't believe how much more work I got done than when I used to have constant interruptions.

The feeling of productivity was so great that I kept at it. A month later, I went back and reviewed my planner and my workload. I had gotten more done in that one month than I had in the last three months! I even had more time to clean out my office space (eliminating clutter made me so much less stressed out and organized), fit in smaller tasks during my down times, and I even got to spend more time with my family, friends and myself.

Originally, I thought that being more productive would limit my time for watching my favorite TV shows or going out for bike rides with my friends, but it turned out that I had even more time for all that. They were so shocked at how much I had changed that I even convinced them to eat healthier and work out with me so that they could see all the incredible benefits. Since I wasn't so burnt out from overloading myself, I even tried out the **80/20** rule—I focused my best on the most important **20%** of my projects and the results were amazing.

You too can make this ultimate change in ***your*** life. The way you do it is completely up to you, but I would highly recommend the advice given in this book. If you are lacking in Energy or just want more, my Ultimate Energy E-Book is a perfect complement to this book. Add extra energy with some determination and willpower, which you can read up more on in my book, Influence, Willpower, and Discipline, and you will soon be doing things you never dreamed possible. The path to get there is worth the hard work, and the feeling you will get from all your many victories will be priceless!

Conclusion

I hope this book was able to help you to help you look at your life from a new perspective to allow you to see how you can improve your productivity and be inspired with plenty of new great ideas.

The next step is to utilize the tips covered in this book and to take immediate action. Write down a goal that you want to accomplish—it could be anything from practicing one of the habits or strategies that we talked about to reevaluating how much time you spend online. Find the closest piece of paper that you have and jot something down. By starting with this goal, you are on your way to living a more productive lifestyle.

Finally, if you discovered at least one thing that has helped you or that you think would be beneficial to someone else, be sure to take a few seconds to easily post a quick positive review. As an author, your positive feedback is desperately needed. Your highly valuable five star reviews are like a river of golden joy flowing through a sunny forest of mighty trees and beautiful flowers! *To do your good deed in making the world a better place by helping others with your valuable insight, just leave a nice review.*

My Other Books and Audio Books
www.AcesEbooks.com

Peak Performance Books

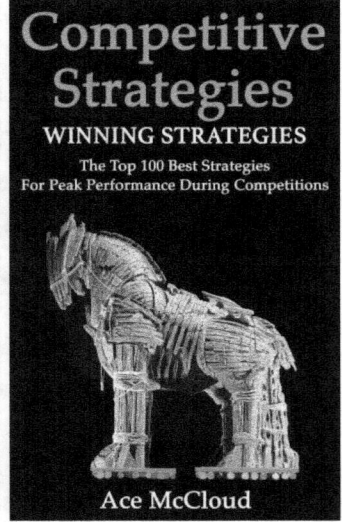

Health Books

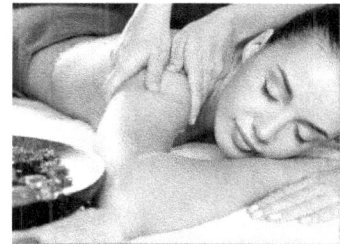

Be sure to check out my audio books as well!

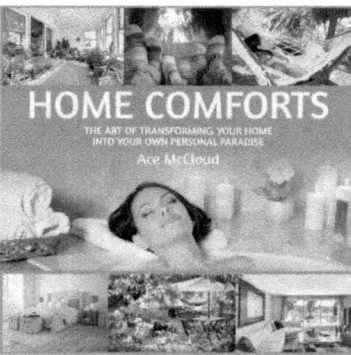

Check out my website at: **www.AcesEbooks.com** for a complete list of all of my books and high quality audio books. I enjoy bringing you the best knowledge in the world and wish you the best in using this information to make your journey through life better and more enjoyable! **Best of luck to you!**

www.ingramcontent.com/pod-product-compliance
Lightning Source LLC
Chambersburg PA
CBHW051429070526
44584CB00023B/3652